CH00847851

Northern Lights, Norway Travel Guide

Sightseeing, Hotel, Restaurant & Shopping Highlights

Rebecca Kaye

If there are any errors or omissions in copyright acknowledgements the publisher will be pleased to insert the appropriate acknowledgement in any subsequent printing of this publication.

Although we have taken all reasonable care in researching this book we make no warranty about the accuracy or completeness of its content and disclaim all liability arising from its use

Table of Contents

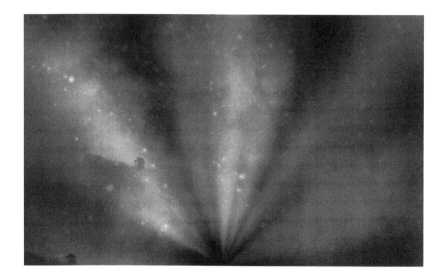

Northern Lights, Norway

For thousands of years people have been fascinated by the Aurora Borealis and its magical display of coloured lights dancing across the northern skies. These northern lights are caused by the earth's magnetic field reacting with electrically charged solar particles. Tromsø in Norway is one of the best places on earth to see this spectacular display.

At an altitude of 60 miles purple or violet lights appear, followed by blue and then turning to red. At the highest point of 150 miles the lights will be greenish in colour. The magnificent formations can appear very rapidly and fill the sky with incredible patterns. The altitude at which this reaction takes place is responsible for the different colours that are seen.

To be successful in seeing nature's very own light show aurora hunters must find somewhere with very little light pollution and clear skies. Tromsø is a great place for Northern Light sightings as in the winter months the city is bathed in a kind of half-light as the sun stays below the horizon all day. The best times to look out for the lights is from around 6pm to midnight as this is when Tromsø moves into the aurora zone due to the Earth's rotation.

For anyone that thinks this part of Norway is only for fishermen and arctic explorers, think again. This bustling city is home to the world's most northernmost university and this alone gives Tromsø a vast student population who love nothing better than having a good time. The numerous bars and restaurants and night-life reflect this and there is always something going on.

The Tromsø population is highly skilled and there is a strong satellite based industry as well as many research institutes. The fishing industry plays a large part in the economy of Tromsø as does the Sámi craftsmen and reindeer herders.

The Norwegians in this part of the country are known for their straightforwardness and sense of humour, many of them speak English and are very welcoming to visitors and love to help. In the main the people are happy and very patriotic. After their native language and English learning a third language is mandatory in Norwegian schools and most students choose French or German and retain the basics of this as adults.

A couple of hundred years ago visitors were amazed to find the city much more civilized than anyone had imagined. With current fashions being worn and a smattering of French being spoken Tromsø earned the nickname the Paris of the North.

Not surprisingly fish features on many menus as does a wide selection of meats, many of which will be completely new to some visitors. Don't be surprised to find whale steak, reindeer meat, shark, seal and elk on the menu. Reindeer is a normal part of the diet and one of the traditional dishes is creamed lappebiff, with lingonberries and mash.

Local soups are tangsuppa made from seafood and seaweed or mølje, a broth made with either fish or meat. There are juicy king-size crab legs, mussels, salted cod and coalfish on menus everywhere as well as the more traditional halibut, cod and haddock.

There are restaurants that serve international menus and it is possible to find vegetarian and gluten free options in some places. Be warned though, it is expensive to eat and drink out in Norway. A meal for two in an average bar or restaurant will set you back around £85 for a couple of main courses, a dessert each and two local beers. A large pizza can cost £30 while a burger can be around a tenner.

Tromsø was a popular place for the start of Arctic expeditions and explorers like Fridtjof Nansen and Roald Amundsen often recruited sailors from the town. In 1940 the city found fame of a different kind when for 38 days it became the capital of Norway.

The city was lucky throughout WWII and avoided any war damage, the closest being the sinking of the German battleship of Tirpitz in November 1944. The Tromsø War Museum tells the story of the city's war history but is only open from May until September.

Culture

In January each year the silver screen comes to Tromsø with Norway's biggest film festival. Since 1991 this week long festival has played host to around 300 screenings, many of them taking place in the main square on a massive screen. The films are selected from around the world and many of them will never have been shown in Norway before. There are also documentaries, short films and silent films to watch as well as talks and quizzes to take part in.

In January and February the musical extravaganza that is the Northern Lights Festival comes to town. Over the past two decades some of the best symphonic orchestras in Scandinavia have performed at this event, which attracts many high profile artists.

In June the Midnight Sun Marathon takes place. Competitors from over 50 nations come to Tromsø to race at night, although due to the midnight sun it is still daylight. There is not just the full marathon but a half-marathon plus a fun run and children's race. To take part pre-registration is necessary.

For beach and music lovers the Bukta Festival takes place in July. The festival is in Telegrafbukta, an incredibly popular camping and swimming spot about a 30 minute walk from the city centre. With never ending daylight in the summer months the festival does live up to the claim of being able to party all day long, due to the fact that there is no night time. The beach is surrounded by trees and mountains and makes a wonderful spot for relaxing and enjoying the music. The artists are not just Scandinavian but many come from the USA as well. There is an excellent website www.bukta.no that gives information. Music lovers can apply via the website to become one of the 500 volunteers that help the festival run smoothly.

Approximately 10% of the population in the county of Troms are of Sámi descent. The Sámi are Europe's oldest surviving culture and many are still reindeer herders yet they integrate well with modern ways and the European way of life. The semi-nomadic lifestyle of the reindeer herders means they follow vast herds from the central highlands in winter to the lowlands in summer, a cycle that has been repeated for thousands of years.

The Sámi also inhabit areas of Finland, Sweden and Russia and out of a population of 100,000 half of these live in Norway. The governments of the countries they inhabit recognise the importance of the Sámi people and how much the freedom of movement means to them. In addition to their language the Sámi have their own government, TV station and educational system.

Location & Orientation

The county of Troms covers around 10,000 square miles and the capital city of Tromsø is the largest Norwegian city north of the Arctic Circle. Tromsø is the eighth largest municipality in Norway and has a population of around 70,000. Another 1300 miles or so further north is the North Pole. Most of the city is on the island of Tromsøya which is connected to the mainland by bridge and tunnel.

Many buildings and businesses in the city are the most northernmost of their kind in the world, the Mack brewery, the Tromsø University and the Botanical Gardens are just three of these. The university and university hospital between them employ approximately three quarters of Tromsø's workforce.

Getting to Tromsø is relatively easy; most international visitors arrive by plane to the small, but modern Langnes airport on the west of Tromsøya. There are domestic flights as well as international ones from the other Scandinavian countries and London Gatwick. To get across the island to Tromsø city centre takes a 15 minute public bus ride that stops just about everywhere or the slightly faster dedicated airport bus. Taxis of course are available but will cost roughly four times the price of a public bus or even more on Sundays.

There are no trains to Tromsø. The nearest railway station is in Narvik, four hours to the south by bus or car. There are also trains from Helsinki to Rovaniemi in Finland which you can take your car on and then cross the border into Norway. Train travel is relatively cheap if you consider the distance travelled so the bus from Narvik to Tromsø will seem expensive in comparison. It is also possible to get the train from Narvik to Sweden.

To travel to the north of Norway by bus will mean going from Tromsø to Alta some 120 miles away and then making connections. To travel south take the bus to Narvik where your journey can be continued by bus or train.

Driving in Norway is fairly easy, even taking into account the snow. The road network is well-maintained and the speed limits are low, particularly in the areas around the fjords. Even if you do not speak Norwegian most petrol stations have excellent travel information and will inform you of any road closures. From Oslo to Tromsø is about a thousand miles and it is worth allowing a few days for the journey to take in the beauty of the country as you travel.

Climate & When to Visit

Tromsø has a subarctic climate as there is a short summer season and the winter temperatures are just cold enough to qualify. The city has a reputation for deep snow in winter and the record so far was in 1997 when a depth of nearly one hundred inches was recorded at the Tromsøya metereological station. Outside of the city there are large areas above the tree line that are classified as having an arctic tundra climate.

Tromsø in winter is not as cold as most would imagine due to the warming effect of the Gulf Stream. The snow does fall heavily and the surrounding landscape turns into a winter wonderland where snow-capped mountains stretch as far as the eye can see.

The winter temperatures reach a high of -1°C and a low of -6°C with a great deal of precipitation. The Polar Night is from November 26th to January 15th when the sun remains below the horizon all day. The return of the sun in the middle of January is a cause for celebration and the nights quickly shorten. By the end of February there is about eight hours of daylight per day which quickly stretches to ten hours by the beginning of April.

The light conditions from the end of February until late April are intense and sunglasses are essential when skiing. By mid-May it is the turn of the Midnight Sun and until mid-August there is no real darkness.

The summer days are long but not necessarily warm. The high is around 14°C while the low is a rather un-summer like 8°C. However, it does save electricity as at midnight in August it is still possible to read outside without a light. The weather varies widely in the summer months, sunny days are interspersed with chilly and drizzly days and overcast skies.

In the summer months the Midnight Sun is the attraction for many visitors and from May 18th to July 26th the sun is always above the horizon. One of the best viewpoints of the city at night is from the Upper Station of the Cable Car. If you don't have a head for heights the views from the front of the Arctic cathedral or from the Tromsø Bridge are also very good.

The spring temperature has a high of 2°C in April rising to about 7°C by the end of May but with lows of -2°C in both months. By October the daytime high is back down to 4°C with a low of zero as winter starts to creep in.

For those seeking the Northern Lights in Tromsø a suitcase full of thermal undies and woollen layers is essential. Cosy, warm and waterproof snow boots or similar footwear will make trips out into the darkness in search of the elusive lights much more bearable. There is no fun in wet, icy cold feet for hours on end. Likewise, pack hats and scarves. A good deal of body heat is lost through the head, so keep it well-covered. Sunglasses, lip balm and high factor sun cream are all good things to pack as well. On top of all these layers a thick padded snow and waterproof jacket and trousers are a must-have. Many of the companies that arrange tours out to chase the Northern Lights and other arctic adventures will provide suitable clothing if you don't have any.

Sightseeing Highlights

Floya Mountain

Fjellheisen
Solliveien 12
N-9020 Tromsdalen
Tel: +47 7763 8737
www.fjellheisen.no

For spectacular views of Tromsø and the surrounding area, take the four minute ride to the top of Fløya Mountain. The creaks and groans of the ancient cable car can be a bit nerve-wracking but it is worth the journey. The cable car drops passengers off at the viewing platform at Storsteinen or Big Rock, just over 2000 feet above sea level.

There are panoramic views of the island framed by the mountains in the distance and everywhere is a winter wonderland. There are different look- out points but snow boots might be needed to reach the best ones through knee deep snow. On New Year's Eve the island and the mainland seem to be in competition with fireworks and dramatic displays in all directions. At midnight though all eyes turn to the top of Big Rock as it bursts into a dazzling light show culminating with the words new year written in fire.

Food is available in the Fjellstua Café with a selection of snacks and light lunches all year around. In the summer months evening meals are served. For anyone with a sweet tooth the café serves svele, a small dense pancake, which is ideal with a warming cup of hot chocolate or coffee.

The cable car runs from 10am to 10pm every day, and until 1am through the Midnight Sun period and on New Year's Eve. Tickets cost £13 for adults and £5 for children.

Arctic Cathedral

Hans Nilsens veg 41
9020 Tromsdalen
Phone: +47 4768 0668
www.ishavskatedralen.no

For anyone that thinks that cathedrals are fusty, dusty places built out of mellowed stone, think again.

The Arctic Cathedral in Tromsø will wipe any thoughts of tradition from your mind with its ultra-modern design. Inspired by Artic nature when it was built in 1965 the cathedral is on the Tromsø mainland by the road bridge across to the island.

The design is unusual but it fits nicely into the stunning mountain scenery. The church is built from aluminum-coated concrete panels and was considered to very daring piece of architecture when it was built in 1965. It has been likened to the Sydney Opera House and it is sometimes called the Opera House of the North. Although referred to as a cathedral this is not strictly true and it is actually a church. The true Tromsø Cathedral is a wooden building and is the only wooden cathedral in Norway.

There have been some additions over the years; in 1972 a glass mosaic depicting the Return of Christ was added to the eastern side. Inside the cathedral the eye is drawn to the magnificent and modern organ, sitting high up in the church. This new organ replaced the old one in 2005 and has 2940 pipes and is quite a splendid sight. It is worth making the effort to see the cathedral at day and also when it is lit up at night. The lighting at night gives the cathedral an eerie blue glow and it is easy to imagine it is made of ice.

In addition to the normal services there are concerts held in the cathedral throughout the year. New Years Eve of course is a very important time but there are also concerts for the Midnight Sun and Midnight Concerts to coincide with the Aurora Borealis and general organ concerts.

The cathedral can be visited in the winter months from 4pm until 6pm and in the summer the hours are much longer. The website has a list of the opening hours. Children are admitted free if they are under 12 and adults pay £4.

Polaria Museum

Hjalmar Johansens gate 12,
9007 Tromsø
Phone: +47 7775 0100
www.polaria.no/

The Polaria Museum is a five minute walk from the city centre and is easy to find. The building has been likened in the past to looking like a knocked over row of dominoes. The huge white slabs are designed to represent the ice floes when they are pressed onto land by rough Artic seas.

In the Arctic aquarium at Polaria the favourite attraction with children and adults is the bearded seals. This arctic species of seal has a very quiet disposition and they are very intelligent. There are many kinds of fish to see as well, a lot of which are native to the Barents Sea.

There is a cinema where visitors can watch short films that tell the history of the Arctic and the effects of the melting ice is having on nature and animals. The film, Svalbard-Arctic Wilderness, takes visitors on a trip through the spectacular scenery and wilderness on Svalbard Island. The archipelago of Svalbard is the most northernmost part of Norway and lies midway between the mainland and the North Pole.

There are many other interesting exhibits to see plus a caféteria and a well-stocked gift shop. The aim of the gift shop is to promote the traditional handcrafts from the people in the Artic and Barents areas as well as selling souvenirs that are related to the museum.

Polaria is open from 10am to 5pm in the winter and from 10am to 7pm in the summer months. An adult ticket costs £12 and there are reductions for children, OAP's, students and family groups.

Coastal Steamer Hurtigruten

Kirkegt 1, Box 6144,
9291 Tromsø
Phone: +47 8100 3030
www.hurtigruten.com/

The Hurtigruten shipping service was originally started by the government in 1893 to improve transport along the rugged and difficult coastline.

Nearly one hundred years later the nature of the ships changed. More emphasis was put on the comfort of passengers and the ships became more luxurious with bars, restaurants and hot tubs. Despite all these modern conveniences Hurtigruten still operates the daily freight and passenger service from Kirkenes in the north to Bergen in the west of Norway. Hurtigruten has a 2% share of the world cruise market.

From Kirkenes to Bergen the round trip journey takes 11 days and is sometimes referred to as the Norwegian Coastal Express. There are many other voyages available and the shortest ones are two to three days. From Tromsø there are sailings north to Kirkenes and passengers can join in the hunt the Northern Lights. This trip in the winter months is a magical experience. The snow clad mountains make a stunning backdrop for the clusters of houses with lights twinkling like fiery embers as you glide past in search of this natural phenomenon.

The Hurtigruten website is comprehensive and gives excellent information on the voyages available and the prices.

Non-Stop Northern Lights Chase

Arctic Guide Service AS – Tromsø, Bankgata 1
N-9008 Tromsø
Tel: +47 9220 7901
www.arcticguideservice.com/

The Arctic Guide Service started in 2001 and now has 130 guides and three management teams to make sure the trips run smoothly. The guides are fluent in nine languages between them, Norwegian and English of course, plus Japanese, Spanish, German, Italian, French, Dutch and Chinese Mandarin. Guides in other languages can be supplied on request.

The Non-Stop Northern Lights Chase runs from September 15th to March 31st every evening. The Aurora Borealis typically appears between 9pm and 1am and the Arctic Guide Service will literally chase the lights trying to find a place with clear skies for the best view. Some of the places can be reached from Tromsø in an hour; some can take two and half hours to reach.

The cost of the trip is £95 per adult with a 50% reduction for children. Proper clothing is essential as it will be very, very cold. Three layers of clothing are recommended with woollen garments being the warmest. Over these layers you will need a decent quality ski jacket and trousers, snow boots, gloves and a hat.

The trips depart at 6.30 pm and returns at 1.30am. The guides constantly check the weather forecasts throughout the trip so they know exactly the right place to head for. Around 45 minutes is spent at each stop waiting for nature's own light show to appear before moving on. For warmth and energy hot drinks and biscuits are provided on the coach between each stop. The guides are very experienced and will explain on the coach all about the lights and how they are formed and many other interesting details.

Science Centre of Northern Norway & Northern Lights Planetarium

Hansine Hansens veg 17
9019 Tromsø
Tel:+ 47 7762 0945.
www.nordnorsk.vitensenter.no/

The Science Centre of Northern Norway started in August 2002 and is located at the University of Tromsø. To get to the Science Centre takes about 40 minutes if you choose to walk from the city centre or there are frequent buses and a large free car park.

There are exhibitions that focus on the conditions in the Arctic, covering everything from climate and weather to the Northern Lights and energy. In the Planetarium there are spectacular short films such as the Origin of Life, Experience the Aurora, Sea Monsters, Our Living Climate, We are Astronomers, Stars and A Magic Northern Lights Night.

The Science Centre and Planetarium works closely in conjunction with local schools and aims to increase the number of students who find science and technology interesting and therefore wish to take these subjects on into further education. There are many activities at the centre that allow local people to join in and learn about today's changes in science and technology.

Opening hours are daily from 11am to 6pm and adults pay £10 and children pay £5.

Whale Island & Reindeer Ride

Tromsø Safari
Sommerlystveien 23
9012 Tromsø
Tel: +47 9751 7583
www.Tromsøsafari.no/

Whale & Killer Whale Safari

The Whale Safari out to the island of Kvaløya takes about five hours and is available from mid-November until mid-January. The boat that is used comes down from Spitsbergen in Svalbad where for the rest of the year it is used for polar bear cruises.

The cruiser can carry up to 120 people and with three spacious decks there is enough room for everybody to get spectacular views of these magnificent creatures. Whales are naturally quite curious and will come close to the boat so there are many photo opportunities. There will also be chances to see sea eagles and seals as well.

The price per adult is £120 and for children under 12 years of age the price is £60.

Reindeer Ride with Sámi Traditional Meal

The Reindeer Ride trip starts at around 9am in the city centre from where you will be driven to a central point and provided with warm clothes. Thermal jackets and trousers will keep you warm and snug on the reindeer sleigh while the boots, hats and gloves make sure that no-one suffers from frost bite of the fingers and toes. When everyone is ready the fun begins as you go to meet the reindeer and their herders.

Sledding through the peaceful Norwegian landscape is an amazing experience and has been the chosen mode of transport for the Sámi people for hundreds of years. The sled ride takes about 30 minutes and in that time the only sounds are the swish of the runners on the crisp snow and the jingle of the reindeer's bells.

The sled ride takes you through scenery usually only found on Christmas cards and afterwards you will return to the lavvo. This typical Sámi reindeer herder's tent might be temporary in nature but none the less it is very secure and weatherproof. By the warmth of the fire coffee is served followed by a bowl of reindeer meat and vegetable soup. The soup is called Bidos and is a Sámi recipe that has been around for many years. The guide will tell you stories about the Sámi way of living and then lessons are given on how to lasso a reindeer.

The Reindeer Ride with the Sámi meal costs £145 for adults and £73 for children under 12. The trip leaves at 9am and lasts for around four to five hours.

Dog Sledding

Villmarkssenter
Straumsvegen 601
9105 Kvaløysletta
Tel: +47 7769 6002
www.villmarkssenter.no/

At the Tromsø Villmarkssenter there are 300 Alaskan huskies of various ages and in different stages of training. The youngest sled dogs at the farm are aged from four weeks to six months and start to go out into the wilderness at a young age to learn their craft.

Alaskan huskies are very people friendly so you can be sure to make some furry friends on a dog sledding trip. During the trip you will learn all about dog sledding and while no experience is necessary, a reasonable level of fitness is required. It is quite possible that as you travel through the pristine Arctic countryside you will see other wildlife. Moose and reindeer are easy to spot but smaller animals like snowshoe and arctic hares, foxes and eagles might be harder to see.

There are different expeditions available; half-day trips can be taken in the afternoon or evening, while the one day trip last eight hours. There are also two and three day dog sledding trips for the more adventurous with overnight stays in a Sámi tent. Whichever trip you choose you will be provided with the appropriate outdoor clothes for protection against the cold and meals and snacks according to the length of the trip.

Regardless of the weather conditions the highly experienced dogs will find a way through the snow covered mountains. There are stunning views looking back down over Tromsø and the fjords in the distance. If the conditions are suitable it is possible to handle your own sled and team of huskies but this must be pre-booked.

Prices vary but for a one day dog sledding trip with meals and outdoor clothes the cost is approximately £250.

Snowshoeing & Cross-Country Skiing

Tromsø Outdoor
Sjøgata 14
9008 Tromsø
Tel: +47 9757 5875
www.Tromsøoutdoor.no/

The season for cross-country skiing and snowshoe activities starts on 1st November and lasts through until the end of March; however this can vary slightly depending on the weather conditions. There are different levels of packages available but the two hours snowshoe and three hours ski tours are very suitable for beginners who have not done this kind of activity before. Children from the age of about eight years are welcome to join in with the snowshoe tour and from about 13 years for the skiing.

The snowshoe or ski tours take place at the top of Tromsøya and after a short transfer from the city centre you will be kitted out with the necessary equipment and set off into the forest. The walk is taken slowly with lots of photo opportunities and your guide will be able to tell you all about the area and the arctic surroundings. There is a break in the tour for a hot drink of blackcurrant and a local treat of lefse. This is a special type of bread with butter and brown cheese or cinnamon.

The cost of the tour includes snowshoes or skis, ski boots and poles, transport from the town and the services of a guide and refreshments. The snowshoe tour is £40 and the ski tour £90

For more adventurous types snowshoes or cross country skis can be hired and with a route map it is possible to set off on your own personal tour. A brief lesson on how to put them and how to use them is included plus advice on the day's weather and where to go. Snowshoes and poles cost about £20 for one day. Cross country skis, poles and boots cost about £28 per day.

Overnight in a Sámi Herdsmen's Tent

Friluftsenter, Risvik
9100 Kvaløysletta
Tromsø
Tel: +47 9075 1583
www.Tromsø-friluftsenter.no

For an amazing experience spend the night in a Sámi tent, surrounded by only nature and a stunning landscape. The trip gives you chance to explore the area through the day and then at night watch out for earth's own stunning lightshow, the Aurora Borealis.

The accommodation is fairly basic, toilets and washing facilities are provided but no showers. The typical reindeer herder's huts have an oven for warmth, and thick sleeping bags on a layer of reindeer skins make for a cosy bed once you have had your fill of the Northern Lights.

The price of the trip is £195 for adults and £97 for children under 12. The price includes one night in a Sámi hut, three meals and transfers to and from the town.

Tromsø Centre for Contemporary Art

Musegata 2, Tromsø 9008
Tel: +47 7765 5827
www.Tromsøkunstforening.no/

The goal of the Contemporary Art Centre is to support
and present contemporary art to locals and visitors alike.
The focus is towards experimental and innovative works
and both new artists and artists of international acclaim
have pieces displayed here. The building that houses the
gallery was built in 1894 and originally was the home of
the Tromsø Museum but when the museum relocated in
the 1980's the Contemporary Art Centre moved in.
Tromsø is the main cultural heart of the north of Norway
and the wonderful art exhibited here with its variety of
styles and themes reflects this.

There is a small bookshop and the Café des Beaux-Arts in
the basement offers a French menu with cakes and lunch
dishes. Entry to the museum is free and opening hours
are midday to 5pm Wednesday to Sunday, closed
Monday and Tuesday.

Tromsø University Museum

Lars Thørings veg 10
9006 Tromsø
Phone: +47 7764 5000
www.uit.no/

The Tromsø University Museum was established in 1872 and is the oldest scientific institution in North Norway and is visited by around 80,000 – 90,000 people every year. There are six departments so whether you prefer geology, insects, indigenous people or Gothic sculpture there is a variety of things to see and do. The collections are varied and the permanent and temporary exhibitions provide many fascinating facts.

The centerpiece of the museum is the nine metre long whale skeleton. Special lighting effects with ever-changing colours make the skeleton look remarkably lifelike. The museum is the largest inside the Arctic Circle and the Sámi exhibition tells the story of how the reindeer herders have made the transition from a traditional lifestyle to living and working with modern ways.

The interactive exhibition on the Northern Lights is great fun where you can make your lightshow on the plasma screen and then take home a souvenir photo. There is a Viking longhouse to explore, plus a caféteria and gift and bookshop. A play and learn area offers opportunities for younger children to get involved and throughout the museum the texts are in both Norwegian and English. There is free parking and the museum is wheelchair friendly.

NORTHERN LIGHTS IN NORWAY TRAVEL GUIDE

Tromsø Museum is open in winter from September to May from 10am to 4.30pm and June to August from 9am to 6pm. Weekend and holiday opening times can be slightly different so it is worth checking before you plan a visit. Entrance fees for adults are £5, children student and OAP's pay £2.50 and under 7's are free.

Art Museum of Northern Norway

Sjogata 1
Tromsø 9008
Tel: +47 7764 7020
www.nnkm.no/

A visit to the Art Museum of Northern Norway will reveal paintings by some surprising names. David Hockney's painting of the Midnight Sun hangs alongside scenes and landscapes by Norwegian artists and on the second floor paintings by Edward Munch represent the 20th century.

The former post office building has examples of Norwegian art with works by Hans Gude, Johan Christian Dahl, Thomas Fearnley and Peder Balke. Other artists include Anna-Eva Bergman, Axel Revold, Jean Heiberg and Lars Tiller.

The three floors of the museum take visitors on a chronological journey showing just how tough life in the Arctic can be and also how beautiful. Many of the paintings feature mountains and fjords plus snowy landscapes captured in every shade of white and grey imaginable.

Entry is free and the museum is open from mid Jun to mid Aug 11am to 6pm and the rest of year 10am to 5pm. Weekends 11am to 5pm.

Recommendations for the Budget Traveller

Places to Stay

AMI Hotel Tromsø

Skolegata 24, 9008 Tromsø
Tel: +47 7762 1000
www.amihotel.no

With 17 rooms and accommodating up to 36 guests the AMI Hotel Tromsø offers a personal and cosy place to stay for a holiday to see the Northern Lights.

The hotel is a few minutes' walk from the main pedestrianised shopping area and there are great views across the town.

There is a good choice of rooms, with single beds for solo travellers to four bedded family rooms, with single or double beds. Basic rooms with just a washbasin are slightly cheaper but en-suite facilities are available. The room rate includes towels, free Wifi and a buffet breakfast with meats, cheeses, breads, cakes, cereals, eggs, jams and all the usual drinks and juices.

There is a guest lounge where tea, coffee and hot chocolate are available free of charge all day, as well as a fully equipped kitchen for cooking any favourite foods. There are computers in the guest lounge as well as TV; Play Stations can be borrowed from reception and there are games, books and magazines to sit down and relax with. The lounges are a great place to meet fellow travellers and swap tales about the Northern Lights.

Each bedroom has a telephone and free calls are available to landlines in several countries including Scandinavia, North America and Western Europe. Parking is easy and free directly outside the hotel. The standard room rates start at £63 for a single room going up to £114 for a room with four beds. Discounts are available for students staying longer than three days.

Sydspissen Hotel

Strandveien 166
9006 Tromsø
Tel: +47 7766 1410
www.sydspissenhotell.no

Sydspissen Hotel is a couple of miles from the centre of Tromsø near the popular beach of Telegrafbukta and Folkeparken. A twenty minute walk will take you from the hotel to the Hålogaland Theatre, the Polaria Tromsø Museum and the Tromsø Music College.

The hotel has 48 rooms, including rooms for disabled visitor. There is a lift; free car parking and children under four years of age stay free. The rooms are all en-suite and have a desk and two chairs if you need workspace. There is a fridge in each room as well as a hospitality tray. Free Wifi is available throughout the hotel, the reception is open 24 hours and offers luggage storage plus breakfast is included in the room rate.

Sydspissen Hotel offers good, clean comfortable accommodation at sensible prices in an excellent location. Single, twin or triple rooms are available and the room rate for a single is £63. Twin and triple rooms work out to about £35 per person per night.

Smart Hotel

Vestregata 7-15
9008 Tromsø
Tel: +47 4153 6500
http://smarthotel.no

The concept of Smarthotel started in 2004 when the first one opened in Norway. The Tromsø Smarthotel opened in 2013 as the demand for reasonably priced and smart accommodation grew in the city. The prices are fixed all year round and the 160 en-suite rooms offer excellent value for money in the heart of the city close to the Arctic Cathedral.

The focus of the Smarthotel is on customer service; from attentive and helpful staff coupled with flexible and comfortable rooms designed to meet the needs of today's travellers. The Smart Mini room is only small with one single bed but it has everything you need for your stay, without wasting space on unnecessary items.

The Smart Double has room for two beds while the Smart Superior gives just a bit more space. The Smart Double and Smart Superior rooms also have a desk and chair.

Whichever room you chose the comfort level will be identical with light-proof blinds, noiseless air-conditioning, free Wifi, flat-screen TV and a high quality bed. The room rates are from £60 for a single to £90 for a twin.

The hotel has 24 hour reception with full service and there are Smart cars and bicycles available for rental. The hotel has a bright airy dining room where a Scandinavian breakfast is available for an extra charge. There is a bar for relaxing in with a selection of carefully chosen wines and beers.

Anemone Bed & Breakfast

Hochlinvegen 21
9008 Tromsø
Tel: +47 7768 6515
www.anemone.skaland.com

The Anemone is a delightful guest house in a lake side setting situated between Tromsø city centre and the airport. The Prestvannet Lake is stunning at any time of the year but particularly in winter when the Northern Lights dance their way across the sky reflected in the cool, clear waters of the lake. In summer the forest areas nearby offer long tracks for nature walks and in winter the same tracks are used as carefully looked after and become well-lit ski tracks.

The Anemone is decorated in typical Scandinavian style with pine panelling in many of the rooms and log fires. Outside there is free parking, ski racks and space to leave bicycles.

There are four bedrooms, two bathrooms and a washing machine is on-site for guests to use. For a small extra charge private facilities are available. The room rate includes towels, bedding, use of the kitchen for preparing light meals and breakfast on your first morning. A single room for one or two nights is around £43 but there are some good discounts for longer stays.

The owner, Oystein and his wife are very welcoming and are more than happy to share their local knowledge with guests. They can suggest all the best places to go to see the Northern Lights and will provide winter suits free of charge to keep you warm. It is a brisk 30 minute walk into the centre of Tromsø but there is a bus stop close by. As the Anemone is in a residential area the light pollution is fairly low so the chances of seeing the lights without leaving the comfy warmth of the guest house are quite good.

St. Elisabeth Hotell Helsehus

Mellomveien 50
9007 Tromsø
Tel: +47 77 75 62 00
www.st-elisabeth.no

Once upon a time the St Elisabeth Hotel had a different function as it used to be the Maternity Hospital in Tromsø.

Nowadays the only sounds in the long corridors are guests on their way to their warm and comfortable rooms, not midwives with starched aprons rustling or babies crying. The hotel is a few minutes' walk from the city centre and from the fifth floor café offers stunning views of the fjords and mountains surrounding the town.

The 24 rooms at the hotel all have free Wifi, private bathrooms, flat-screen TV with cable channels, a desk and electrically adjustable beds. A double room for one night is about £87, not including breakfast but various deals are available. The reception desk is open from 8am to 10.30pm seven days a week but arrangements can be made with the hotel for late arrivals. There is a ski storage room, a laundry room, a fully equipped kitchen for guests to use and free hot drinks available all day long. For some relaxation therapy the indoor pool is comfortably heated to 32° C and there are spa, sauna and fitness facilities.

The hotel is clean and the staff are helpful and informative. For a small extra charge there is an excellent breakfast buffet with cereals, meats, cheese, fish, fruits and yogurts, breads and cakes. There are panoramic views from the dining room windows as the surrounding buildings are lower than the hotel. Lunch is also served at the hotel but there are many options close by for guests wishing to dine out.

Places to Eat & Drink

Peppes Pizza

Stortorget 2
Tromsø
Tel: +47 2222 5555.
www.peppes.no

It was a lucky day for pizza-eating Norwegians when in 1970 an American by the name of Louis Jordan moved to Oslo. Jordan had for many years run a small pizza restaurant in Connecticut but with his Norwegian wife they decided to make the move back to her home country. Jordan opened his first restaurant in Oslo and Peppes Pizza was born. The unique taste of the tomato sauce used has been the secret of the restaurants success and although many have tried to replicate the delicious taste of herbs and spices, no-one has succeeded.

The successful chain now is the market leader in Norway for pizza restaurants and has over 2,500 employees from Hammerfest to Kristiansand. 22,000 meals a day or 4 million pizzas a year tell their own story. The range has widened and now there are folded pizzas as well as the traditional flat ones, gluten-free pizzas, burgers, salads and soft drinks.

The restaurants are open daily from 11am to 11.30pm and a basic 30cm cheese and tomato pizza is around £13. There is a lunchtime daily special menu and this is one of the best ways to introduce yourself to a Peppes Pizza.

Gründer

Storgata 44
Tromsø
Tel: +47 7775 3767

If you love chocolate fondant and ice cream for dessert this is definitely the place to go to. For main meals there is an international style menu with items such as roasted cod or mussels in wine sauce, plus all kinds of salads, snacks and sandwiches.

There is a good feeling in Gründer and the service is informal and as evening falls the bar does get busy, especially at weekends when a party like atmosphere prevails. The restaurant opens at 11am and service carries on through into the evenings.

Vertshuset Skarven

Strandtorget 1
Tromsø
Tel: +47 7760 0728
http://skarven.no

Vertshuset Skarven is a selection of places to eat and drink by the waterfront in Tromsø owned by the same group. Skarven Kro is a pub open from 11am every day where light lunches and dinners are served and Skarven Bar opens just in the evenings for drinks. For dining out Arctandria and Biffhuset are the fish and meat restaurants respectively.

Arctandria Seafood Restaurant opens at 4pm Monday to Saturday and is frequented by locals and visitors alike. Situated on the waterfront the top floor of this old warehouse has been converted into a super restaurant where candlelight softens the interior and adds a touch of romance.

The whole menu is fish, and not just any fish but the best and freshest fish imaginable. For 25 years the most popular dish has been the fillet of stockfish grilled with garlic butter and served with stewed carrots, potatoes and bacon. There is a whole range of familiar and some more unusual dishes to try. The starters include savoury fish roe or mussels, or maybe a carpaccio of whale meat. Main courses of Arctic shark meat with pepper sauce or Arctic char with hazelnuts make a change from beef or salmon.

The Lutefisk buffet at £46 is very popular. Lutefisk is made from white fish, normally cod, with the addition of lye in a quite complicated series of steps that take several days. The end result is a gelatinous mass that has an incredibly strong smell. The cooked Lutefisk is served with a variety of sauces and vegetables that vary from place to place. Leftover Lutefisk should always be cleared away; as if it is left overnight the sticky substance is almost impossible to remove. Another word of warning is to use stainless steel implement, never, ever sterling silver.

Biffhuset Steakhouse serves all kinds of steaks and meat dishes, not just the usual beef, but Arctic reindeer, Arctic grouse and whale steak are on the menu along with seal lasagne. There is also a good choice of goat, lamb, pork and chicken. Biffhuset opens seven days a week from 3.30pm.

Driv

Søndre Tollbodgata 3b
9008 Tromsø
Tel: +47 7760 0776

Driv is a student run restaurant in a converted warehouse but the meaty burgers are to die for, especially the famous Driv burger. There is a wide choice of other salads and snacks as well as interesting items like reindeer pizza. There are several different levels, the first two being part of the café and the top two being used for concerts and events. For anyone that is feeling adventurous there is an open-air hot tub. Driv is open from noon to 6pm mid-June to mid-August and 2pm to 2am the rest of the year.

Knoll og Tott

Storgata 62
9008 Tromsø
Tel: +47 7766 6880

For a reasonably priced meal or a snack Knoll og Tott is a good place to go.

There is a range of 14 baguettes to choose from and 11 salads. There are also homemade lasagnes and jacket potatoes for a more filling lunch. The smell of the bread baking as you wait for you meal will make your mouth water in anticipation and everything is prepared on the premises. The staff are friendly and meals can be eaten in or taken away. Knoll og Tott is open Monday to Friday 10am to 6pm and Saturday 10am to 4pm.

Places to Shop

Nerstranda

Nerstranda 9
9008 Tromsø
Tel: +47 7765 3700
www.nerstranda.no

Nerstanda is a shopping centre in the heart of Tromsø. There are around 46 shops to choose from with well-known names such as Jack Jones, Bijou Brigitte and Accessorize. There is a large health food store where supplies of skin care, minerals and vitamins can be purchased as well as a range of healthy option foods.

Caféteria's and a sushi restaurant offer a variety of meals and snacks for hungry shoppers to rest weary feet and replenish energy reserves. A specialist tea and coffee store has a tempting range of goods for making the best hot drink in city as well as a delightful smelling selection of herbs and spices.

There is fashion for all the family, a hairdresser, an opticians plus a florists that supports Fair Trade and a card and book shop.

Nerstranda is open Monday to Saturday 10am to 8pm, with slightly earlier closing on Thursday and Saturday at 6pm.

Storgata

The main shopping street in Tromsø is on the island part of the city and is called Storgata. This pretty pedestrianised street with its brightly coloured shops and houses is a delightful place to shop and mix with the locals. For small home items try Britt's Boutiques, while Bokhuset Libris has local guide books as well as postcards and maps. The electrical shop of JM Hansen has been around since 1925 and has some of the beautiful examples of Nordic and modern lighting as well as other decorative items.

There are many design shops selling traditional handicrafts and modern Scandinavian jewellery as well as the fine arts from northern Norway's native Sámi people. Don't miss the opportunity to find a few Arctic fishy delicacies or maybe some reindeer meat. In general opening hours are Monday to Friday 9am to 6pm and 7pm on Thursday, Saturday 10am to 4pm and closed on Sunday.

Tromsø Market

From the market square in Tromsø there is a super view of the Arctic cathedral, the cable car and the mountains. In the summer the colourful parachutes of the extreme sports lovers can be seen against the lush greenness, in winter the sun bounces off the brilliant white snow.

The market square or Torget is a very important space in any Norwegian town, where the community gathers at Christmas to dance and sing carols and at other times of the year for festivals and public ceremonies. Any time of the year the market will be in the square with the freshest catch of the day available as well as Norwegian wool products, Sámi crafts and other trinkets.

In winter months look out for the Smultring stall, similar to a donut these heavy dough rings are fried in lard and best eaten piping hot as the grease drips everywhere. At Christmas time on Saturdays there will be a gløgg stall. This traditional drink is warmed over an open fire and served with raisins, almonds and pepperkake, a ginger flavoured biscuit.

Blast

Peder Hansensgate 4, Tromsø 9008
Tel: +47 7768 3460
www.blaast.no/

Blast is the most northerly glass blowing factory in Norway and as far as anyone knows in the whole world.

A few steps away from Storgata and the shops these dedicated and imaginative workers keep warm by the furnaces practicing the centuries old craft of glass-blowing. The glassware is intriguing, from pretty tumblers and wineglasses in clear and coloured glass to earrings and miniature glass lorries.

 A visit to the factory doesn't take long and make sure not to go at noon when the glassblowers are at lunch. At other times visitors are more than welcome to watch as these delicate items are created in front of them. The staff are friendly and have time and patience to explain the process and answer any questions.

There is a small shop where these beautiful and original pieces can be purchased at very reasonable prices as a reminder of your stay in Tromsø. The opening hours are Monday to Friday 10am to 5pm and Saturday 10am to 3pm.

Tromsø Gift & Souvenir Shop

Strandgata 36, 9008 Tromsø
Tel: +47 7767 3413
www.tgss.no

Tromsø Gift and Souvenir Shop, or TGSS has a wonderful selection of gifts and products to choose from all made in the local areas.

Norse mythology, the Vikings, Sámi and coastal culture exist very strongly in and around Tromsø and this is reflected in the goods on sale here. Many of the items are hand-made and some of the ranges from the polar regions are extremely popular and demand outweighs supply.

The aim of the shop is promote local craftsmen and locally designed clothes and knitwear, jewellery and porcelain gifts fill the shelves of this Aladdin's cave of souvenirs. Some gifts are typically Norwegian, like moose, trolls and bears. There are also knives and pelts, beautifully carved wooden bowls and leather bags and rucksacks.

The shop is only about 100 metres or so from the waterfront in Tromsø and is open Monday to Saturday from 10am to 6pm in the winter with longer hours in the summer months when it is open on Sunday afternoons as well.

9064523R00030

Printed in Great Britain
by Amazon.co.uk, Ltd.,
Marston Gate.